NEW ORLEANS
LIFE AND DEATH IN THE BIG EASY

NEW ORLEANS
LIFE AND DEATH IN THE BIG EASY

CHERYL GERBER
Foreword by Lolis Eric Elie
Essay by Chris Rose

2015
University of Louisiana at Lafayette Press

ISBN 13 (paper): 978-1-935754-70-1

http://ulpress.org
University of Louisiana at Lafayette Press
P.O. Box 40831
Lafayette, LA 70504-0831

Printed on acid-free paper in China.

Library of Congress Cataloging-in-Publication Data

Gerber, Cheryl.
New Orleans : life and death in the Big Easy / Cheryl Gerber ; foreword by Lolis
Eric Elie ; essay by Chris Rose.
pages cm
Includes bibliographical references.
ISBN 978-1-935754-70-1 (paper : acid-free paper)
1. New Orleans (La.)--Pictorial works. 2. New Orleans (La.)--Social life and
customs--Pictorial works. 3. New Orleans (La.)--Social conditions--Pictorial works.
4. City and town life--Louisiana--New Orleans--Pictorial works. I. Rose, Chris,
1960- II. Title.
F379.N543G46 2015
976.3'35--dc23
                                                    2015023651:

UL PRESS
UNIVERSITY OF LOUISIANA AT LAFAYETTE PRESS

Remain true to yourself, but move ever upward toward greater consciousness and greater love! At the summit you will find yourselves united with all those who, from every direction, have made the same ascent. For everything that rises must converge.

French philosopher
Pierre Teilhard de Chardin

Boy rides bike in St. Joseph Cemetery No. 1 (2014).

LIFE AND DEATH IN THE BIG EASY

by
Chris Rose

Irony is more than a simple twist of fate in New Orleans.

In New Orleans, irony is a birthright. It's our original sin, the mark of the beast which identifies and binds us as a tribe for all of our days.

It's the one immutable strand of DNA in our shared cultural gene pool so resistant to change, not even Marie Laveau could have broken its hold with her spells, potions, and incantations.

Like our faith, it is unshakable.

Call it the American curse: Irony has marked every occasion of historical and cultural significance to the city since Louisiana joined the Union in 1812.

Take that war, for instance. Its culminating event was the Battle of New Orleans, when British troops made landfall just south of the city with every expectation of swift conquest. They were slaughtered by a ragtag assembly of soldiers, mercenaries, and privateers.

And, depending on your theological inclinations, the intercession of Our Lady of Prompt Succor, to whom the nuns at the Ursuline Convent in the French Quarter prayed during an all-night vigil the night before the battle.

That was in January of 1815. One of the bloodiest battles of the war. And a moot point it all was. Because in December of 1814, the British had surrendered at a meeting of the two nations in Belgium.

Seems like somebody didn't get the memo. Including Our Lady.

Then there's the state song of Louisiana, "You Are My Sunshine." Everybody knows it. In Louisiana, folks love it hard. Gov. Jimmie Davis won office twice, two decades apart, by singing it at campaign rallies around the state and making people feel good about themselves and their home, while his opponents did nothing but talk about problems.

What nobody realized then—and for that matter, now—is that Davis didn't write that song. Nor did anybody else from Louisiana. It was written by a guy from Georgia. And there's not a single word in it about Louisiana. No reference to anything we do here, nor anything that happens here.

Other than the sun shining every now and then. But in the song, that's just a metaphor.

In 2005, Hurricane Katrina bore down on New Orleans the week of Southern Decadence, the largest gay pride event in the South. The annual drag parade that highlights the festival draws more than 150,000 people into the French Quarter to sashay and preen.

The levees broke the Monday before the event, inundating the city with floodwater. Decadence organizers cancelled the event and fled the city. A stunned nation struggled to determine the extent and cause of the damage.

On that Wednesday, this statement from the website *Repent America* was typical of the sentiments of hundreds of other conservative websites, preachers, and radio hosts who wasted no time apportioning blame:

> *Southern Decadence has a history of filling the French Quarter section of the city with drunken homosexuals engaging in sex acts in the public streets and bars. This act of God destroyed a wicked city. New Orleans that had its doors wide open to the public celebration of sin. From the devastation may a city full of righteousness emerge.*

In the following days, as a fuller picture of that devastation emerged, the news was dire: Eighty percent of the buildings in New Orleans were either damaged or destroyed. One of the few areas that neither flooded nor sustained extensive wind damage was the French Quarter, home to the highest concentration of gay residents and businesses in the city—and Southern Decadence.

Men kiss in reaction to anti-gay protests in the French Quarter (2003).

Chris Rose

On that Sunday, two dozen men independently found their way to Bourbon Street, some in dresses dripping wet from floodwaters they forged to get there. Marching under a torn and tattered rainbow banner, they had themselves a righteous parade.

Then there's Louis Armstrong, the musician most intrinsically linked to New Orleans—the face, the voice, and the sound of this city. Our airport and our biggest Downtown park are named after him. His face seems to be on half the souvenirs sold in the French Quarter.

But here's the thing about Louis Armstrong, Mr. New Orleans, our international ambassador of spirit and song. When he was twenty-one years old, he moved to Chicago to join King Oliver's Creole Jazz Band. And he never lived in New Orleans again.

He did, however, come back to be King of the Zulu parade once.

That New Orleans seized upon Satchmo to be the entirety of its tourism and marketing campaign through the 1950s, 60s, and 70s tells a lot about who and what we are.

In New Orleans, our saving grace is that we get it all wrong in just the right way.

The French Quarter is composed almost entirely of Spanish architecture. The official website for New Orleans is CityofNO.com, and City Hall occupies Perdido Street, which is Spanish for lost, and anyone who ever conducted business with the city understands why this is.

All transactions and activities here are marked by contrast, contradiction, or coincidence. Or all three. The general state of affairs is incongruity. Or, as the famous line from the movie *JFK* goes: "It's a riddle wrapped in a mystery inside an enigma."

That *JFK* was set and filmed in New Orleans is merely coincidence.

New Orleans's unique geographical setting is hardly a salve for the paradox of living here. For starters, the city is completely surrounded by water, on all sides, in every direction. Yet there is none you can drink and nowhere to swim.

The Mississippi River plays a particularly keen trick upon the eyes and mind: At varying points around the city, depending where you are standing, the river can be seen, respectively, to the North, the East, the South, and the West.

But it gets worse. Or better, depending on your disposition about such matters.

Life and Death in the Big Easy

There are legions of commuters, for instance, who leave their neighborhood in East Jefferson every morning and drive due South—across the river—to the West Bank. After work, it's a straight shot North back to East Jefferson. Which is about ten miles West of New Orleans East.

It's exhausting just reading that. Imagine the existential toll such a journey like that exacts from your sensory perception over a lifetime. A commute like that informs the kind of person who—when they get flustered—says "I don't know which way is up."

And they mean it.

A lot of this might explain how, for the thirty years I have lived in New Orleans, I've watched a whole lot of people around here moving real fast but going nowhere.

It's a paradox and a challenge living here, but also a triumph of the human spirit. After Katrina, we took a broken, sodden wasteland—given up on by the vast majority of Americans—and built it back into a city full of righteousness indeed.

It is a place unlike any other, where oddity is normal, variation is standard, and eccentricity is not just tolerated, but celebrated.

Of the many shared obsessions among residents here—food, music, hospitality—perhaps none has a stronger and stranger grip than death.

Coming into the city from the airport—and all destinations to the North and West—the first sight to greet the visitor to New Orleans is a vast, seemingly endless horizon of tombs, crypts, and mausoleums. They are truly Cities of the Dead, miles of cemeteries lining both sides of the highway, serving as a literal gateway into New Orleans.

Those above-ground cemeteries and a dozen more around the city are among our most popular tourist destinations. Every now and then you'll happen upon a tomb defaced with X's and other symbols, with offerings of cash, rum, herbs, or tobacco on the ground. These forbidden tchotchkes may or may not indicate the remains of a resident once fluent in the dark arts; urban mythology has a way of creating its own star maps—particularly here in the place they now call "Hollywood South."

On All Saints and All Souls Days, tradition impels thousands of residents to descend upon the cemeteries with picnic baskets and paintbrushes in hand to whitewash the family crypts and signal the start of a New Year on the necromantic calendar. The literal descendants spread checkered tablecloths

Chris Rose

on top of tombs and feast, in both Catholic and secular fashion, visiting with cemetery neighbors they see but this one time a year.

From the moment you arrive in this city and observe these traditions, you know you are not in Kansas—or anywhere else—anymore. We do things a little differently here, including grieve.

As the saying here goes: New Orleans puts the "fun" in funeral.

And it's true: With all the drinking, dancing, smoking, and general carrying on attendant to the interments of the city's musicians, minor celebrities, and generally colorful characters, they're often a better time than weddings. First off, there's considerably less anxiety and mistrust among family members about with whom the dearly departed will be spending all their time now.

And you don't need an invitation to go to a funeral in New Orleans.

And the bands are almost always better.

⚜   ⚜   ⚜   ⚜

Lindy Boggs funeral (2013).

Life and Death in the Big Easy

Back in August of 2005, headlines across the nation pronounced unequivocally: "The Death of an American City." But reports of our demise were premature speculation—or misplaced wishful thinking.

There was no death of an American city; it was instead the drowning of an American Dream. Everything changed in that moment for everyone. But New Orleans didn't die because we who live here—dependent upon the kindness of a lot of strangers out there in this great nation—wouldn't let it. And we never will, the unironic ministrations of *Repent America* and its ilk notwithstanding.

You can't beat down a people who parade in tragedy, dance at funerals, and love among the ruins. Like the Mardi Gras Indian chant goes: "Won't bow down/Don't know how."

It's because of things like that: the legions of black men who don elaborate tribal headdress and stalk each other through the streets on St. Joseph's Night to confront in ritualistic showdowns—and shout-downs—over who is the "prettiest."

Because Jews here decorate Christmas trees in December and Italians wearing green pants parade through the Irish Channel on St. Patrick's Day, handing out paper flowers in return for kisses from strangers.

And float riders toss cabbages, carrots, and onions to the crowds so they can make stew.

Because—in a city beleaguered by more poverty, blight, and homelessness than most—the city's richest men come together once a year to throw millions of dollars of cheap plastic baubles and trinkets from up high on opulent floats to the outstretched hands of the masses gathered below.

Let *them* eat King Cake.

Because—of the two true broadcast legends in this town—one had a speech impediment worse than the other.

Because cab drivers here call you Babe. Doesn't matter if they're male or female nor which you are. Everybody here calls you Babe. And you can call them Babe back and nobody gets mad.

Babe, Babe, Babe! Try *that* in New York City.

Because the best po-boy in New Orleans is made by a Hispanic woman in a Cajun grocery owned by Koreans in a black neighborhood.

Because no other city smells like sweet olive, coffee, mule shit, fish fry, and sex.

Because we are by turns unaware, unconcerned, or unconvinced of our own mortality. Because we are sure, and bound together, by our own morality. Because the longer you live in New Orleans, the more unfit you become to live anywhere else.

Chris Rose

And because the Ursuline nuns are still here. We've got Our Lady of Prompt Succor on our side for whatever battle comes next, whatever may threaten the delicate balance between our comedy and tragedy, our tolerance and negligence, our laughter and forgetting.

Even if she does get it a little wrong sometimes, it always comes out all right.

St. Roch neighborhood (2014).

FOREWORD

by
Lolis Eric Elie

Forget about the South. Think, for a moment, only of New Orleans.

There will be plenty of time and reason to remember the South in the coming paragraphs. But at this point, your vision—our vision—of the Jim Crow South is such a straitjacket of rigid lines and northern constructions, that it cannot possibly accommodate the reality of New Orleans.

In 1803, we were sold up the river in what New Orleans filmmaker Dawn Logsdon has come to refer to as the "American Purchase." Our country kin came to New Orleans to teach us English and the other finer points of capitalist civilization. But a funny thing happened on the way to the bank. The Americans became Creolized.

The krewe of Comus was a gang of Confederate thugs. Their 1877 Carnival parade and ball were dedicated to "The Aryan Race." But—and for our purposes here this is the important part—the platform they used to express their views was the Carnival, a European celebration brought to Louisiana by Bienville and virtually unknown in the Anglo-Saxon outposts in North America. Much of that Puritan foolishness about hard work and thrift gave way to New Orleanian values of celebration and (relative) tolerance.

In recounting his experiences in Rio de Janeiro, Orson Welles observed in the *New York Post* in 1945, "Wherever the moneychangers have taken over, Carnival is no more. Wherever work is so hard that a holiday means rest instead of a good time, Carnival is only a word for a tent show."

Here the moneychangers fell in with the out crowd. The stiff upper lip proved flexible.

Make no mistake. Prejudice in New Orleans was homicidal and strict. But in *Vendetta*, a book about the 1891 lynching of several Sicilian immigrants, Richard Gambino quotes a pair of passages from New Orleans newspapers suggesting that a strong culture ran counter to our assumptions about how race was lived in this place in that period. "In our daily walks through life we notice the surprising amount of co-habitation of white men with Negro women," the *New Orleans Lantern* reported on May 22, 1888. "This thing of white girls becoming enamored of Negroes is becoming rather too common," the *New Orleans Mascot* wrote on November 30, 1889.

Far more pervasive than such couplings were integrated neighbor-

AT LEFT: *Boys playing Downtown (2007).*

hoods. Residential patterns in New Orleans were more integrated two decades before the Civil Rights Act of 1964 than they were two decades after
it. In Carrollton, the uptown neighborhood where I grew up in the 1970s,
there were welfare recipients around one corner and well-heeled matrons
around another. At the end of the block was a woman with a barking collie
who taught swimming lessons, but to "whites only."

But be careful what you conclude. The white Italians lived on the welfare side of things and seemed little more affluent than their darker neighbors. Though we didn't swim together, we did live next to one another. There
was a bit of play in the lines that separated us. In every "bad" part of town,
there was a "good" part of town just a few blocks away.

The people placed side by side in Cheryl Gerber's photographs may
never have met in real life. But their real lives must be combined and considered in any full portrait of their city. Gerber weaves together a story of
this place that focuses on our connectedness, and looking through Gerber's
context we see connections we might otherwise miss. A black woman with
an impossibly stiff hairdo seems less like "the Other" when her photograph
is placed next to one of a white woman with her own sprayed-in-place coif
standing at a fundraiser for the ballet.

While much is made of racial divide, Gerber is just as concerned with
issues of class. Her photographs demonstrate that, whether you stayed in
New Orleans during Hurricane Katrina or evacuated to higher ground, you
found yourself waiting in a long line. Whether you are a homeless New
Orleanian or a migrant worker who came to help the city recover from the
failure of the federal levees, you were likely to find yourself in a small tent
living virtually outdoors. Whether water for you means recreation or disaster,
it is an unavoidable element in the Crescent City.

These photographs are full of symbols, but Gerber knows that any
symbol has more than one meaning. The American flag of the Korean War
veterans on Veterans Day is not the American flag of the Mardi Gras Indian on the first anniversary of Hurricane Katrina. The flag doesn't mean the
same thing in the free community health clinic as it does at a rally to protest
President Obama's health care bill. The National Guardsman and the Lady
Buckjumper both wear camouflage.

By pairing these photographs, Gerber has created a new narrative. But
the power of the pairings is made possible by the underlying story in the in-

Lois Eric Elie

dividual photographs. Looking at the two men dancing at a demonstration to save Charity Hospital, you are impressed at the way Gerber has coordinated their steps. Paired with the dancing boys with their fake teeth on the other page, the bi-racial element in each photo resonates more fully. The picture of the Lucky Dog vendor manning his cart on Bourbon Street is a great occupational portrait of a New Orleans icon. But it is brought into fuller satirical focus by the faux "Sucky Dogs" vendor and the phallic iconography of the Carnival parade on the adjoining page.

These photographs, separated in some instances by more than a decade, are testimony to the enduring culture of New Orleans. Even in the aftermath of the largest government-enabled disaster ever on American soil, the spirit of New Orleans maintains much of what it embodied before Hurricane Katrina. The camera still loves this place, and Cheryl Gerber demonstrates the beauty that can emerge when that love is coupled with technical skill and a great eye.

Girls playing Uptown (2013).

Girl on St. Charles Avenue Streetcar (2007).

PHOTOGRAPHER'S NOTES

by
Cheryl Gerber

I still remember the first time that I became aware of an African American family. My mother and I boarded the Magazine Street bus in New Orleans, Uptown near Napoleon Avenue where we lived. "Don't stare," my mother whispered, as I peered over the back of my seat. "They are just like us," she said. But in my four-year-old mind, I perceived a striking difference.

A year after that memorable bus ride, my family moved to the suburbs, part of the White Flight that forever changed New Orleans.

A few years later, my flamboyant uncle—the father of my six cousins—"came out of the closet" causing mass hysteria in our family. Shortly afterward, we made a sudden exodus to then-rural Northshore, even further from the brilliance and diversity of New Orleans. One hour and a world away from the city where I was born, I experienced a fine, if somewhat lackluster childhood, isolated from virtually any cultural diversity. Sure, there were some African American kids and possibly a couple of gay students, but we didn't mingle outside of the schoolyard.

Eager to expand my horizons, yet fearful of the extreme change, I studied journalism at Southeastern Louisiana University. When college was over, I got a job as an editorial assistant at *New Orleans Magazine* and moved back to New Orleans where I discovered the amazing documentary photography of Michael P. Smith. I pestered him until he finally let me carry his equipment and work in his darkroom. My world suddenly opened up.

During my time working with Mike, my curiosity about other cultures and people deepened, and I began to make connections with them through the lens. As the years passed, my professional work for newspapers and magazines took me right inside the worlds of the rich and poor, the black and white, the good and the bad, the exotic and mundane—all within my rediscovered hometown.

I've taken many photographs of New Orleanians during the past twenty-five years, yet the idea for this book almost eluded me. One day, while reviewing my work on my computer screen, two random photos from two different years leapt out at me: a photo I shot of a secondline parade of an African American woman with a bleached-blonde hairstyle rising several inches above her crown and one of a prominent socialite dressed for a Marie

Antoinette-themed fundraiser with a very similar 'do. "Only in New Orleans," I chuckled.

The idea of *New Orleans: Life and Death in the Big Easy* was born. Much to my amazement, I sighted many more such pairings of pictures, and while each alone was interesting, as a group, they became poignant.

As I delved deeper into my archives, dozens more of these juxtapositions began to surface, reflecting racism, classism, and the economic disparity that sometimes overshadows the beauty of New Orleans—white children leaping into a bright blue pool; black children jumping onto thrown-away mattresses in front of a blighted house.

Because of my own prejudices and fears of being misunderstood, I was worried that these photos would project a cynical or at least a pessimistic tone. To my bewilderment, I have found them neither sarcastic nor pessimistic, but rather a humorous and sometimes painful account of the dichotomies of our culture and the contradictions that make life and death here both joyful and sorrowful, much like the process of creating this book.

I never photographed a single photo with *New Orleans: Life and Death in the Big Easy* in mind. But once the concept became apparent, I realized how many aspects of my photography mirror my own life in New Orleans. I live on a street that seemingly separates blacks and whites, haves and have-nots, and gay and straight couples. I ride a streetcar on a track that separates the opulent Garden District and the dilapidated Central City. I live in a house spared by the water line of Katrina, but that did not spare my friends and neighbors. I live in a city where I'm awakened regularly by gunshots, but I rarely know the victims, who live only a few blocks away.

I would lie awake many nights remembering one pairing after another. I would jump out of bed and search frantically for my photo of the Black Men of Labor to match the shipyard workers that I photographed years earlier, or the archbishop in his pink robe and staff matched with a drag queen dressed in pink as "Little Bo Peep."

Other times I awoke in horror remembering a connection between two photos. Such a pairing included a photo I shot of the vigil for Wendy Byrne, the beloved French Quarter bartender who was shot dead by young teens during a botched robbery in 2009. I shot the photo of mourners on the spot where Wendy died, just a few blocks from my home. I wasn't on assignment but attended the vigil as a neighbor. It wasn't the first time I attended a vigil for a slain neighbor. In 1996 I lived two blocks from site of the infamous Louisiana Pizza Kitchen murders, when three employees were shot to death, another left dying. The bitter sweetness of finding such a familiar scene separated by a few blocks and several years still haunts me.

Cheryl Gerber

In my saddest moments, when I believe I just can't take life in New Orleans another minute, suddenly like a flash, a magical moment seems to come out of nowhere, changing the entire outlook. One eerily quiet Sunday afternoon, my car broke down on the "wrong side of town," in a notoriously dangerous neighborhood. The tow guy said he would be there in forty-five minutes. A lot could happen in forty-five minutes I thought, as my mind reeled over several scary scenarios.

I sat in my locked car and could hear some commotion stirring around the corner. I instinctively hit the power locks again when, out of the blue, came dancing men in lavender suits, transforming the entire complexion of things.

Most of the material in this book covers several years before and after Hurricane Katrina, the storm that dealt the city the biggest blow in its history.

Besides the obvious physical devastation, Katrina took its toll on race relations as talk of shrinking the city's footprint caused a firestorm of reaction. Mayor Nagin's "Chocolate City" speech and the demolition of the city's Big Four housing projects widened the divide between the races. There was talk of New Orleans becoming a "boutique" city. Rich developers were met with angry resistance to the idea of turning entire neighborhoods into green space.

But when I began this book five years ago, I began to see glimmers of hope for New Orleans. I looked at the photo of my then-six-year-old nephew and his best friend, who he calls his brother, which I snapped as they danced down the street during a sleepover. We were on our way to a St. Joseph's Day parade to celebrate the Italian holiday in the French Quarter, and they insisted on dressing alike. (They got the teeth at another parade.)

During the parade, they danced together to the delight of camera-toting tourists, obviously intrigued by the sight of a black boy and a white boy dancing together in the nearly three-hundred-year-old streets of the once, and not-too-long-ago, segregated *Vieux Carre*. At the end of their performance, the street erupted in wild applause. They immediately started making plans for their newfound stardom and made up their stage name "The Dancing Brothers," clueless to the novelty of their spectacle.

It felt like the first time in my life race didn't matter. Our red state had just put the nation's first Indian-American governor in office, our predominantly black city had just elected its first white mayor in more than thirty years, and our majority white country elected its first black president, who invited our first Vietnamese congressman to watch the Super Bowl in the White House. And if that were not enough, the perennially hapless Saints won!

Photographer's Notes

I was on Bourbon Street when the New Orleans Saints became world champions. Rich, poor, black, white, young, and old spilled onto the famous street as euphoria swept in a new day in a new New Orleans. In many ways, New Orleans is a much different city than it was when the levees failed.

More recently, *Forbes Magazine* called us the "Brain Gain," as thousands of young, smart people are flooding the city with new ideas and energy. Newcomers are discovering a New Orleans that many, like myself, took for granted.

I was amazed when HBO came to down to film David Simon's *Treme*. I photographed beloved trumpeter Kermit Ruffins for *Gambit*, and I asked him a question, his reply to which I will never forget. "Kermit, did you ever dream in your life that HBO would be doing a story on your neighborhood and you would be playing yourself?!" His very nonchalant reply: "Oh, I always knew."

⚜   ⚜   ⚜   ⚜

Little girl in Lower 9th Ward photographs Angelina Jolie and Brad Pitt (2007).

Cheryl Gerber

It has not been an easy ten years. When times were really tough, I would always think of the quote from nineteenth-century writer Lacfadio Hearn. "Times are not good here. The city is crumbling into ashes. It has been buried under taxes and frauds and maladministrations so that it has become a study for archaeologists . . . but it is better to live here in sackcloth and ashes than to own the whole state of Ohio." No offense to Ohio.

Ten years after Katrina, scars remain, but there is a sense of possibility unthinkable a decade ago. Yet for many still trying to return, rising rents and gentrification have made it impossible for many homecomings.

As the city struggles to rebuild and redefine itself, many believe that the future in New Orleans could be a model of what's possible to turn around a once decaying American city. I just hope that that bright future is not just for *some* New Orleanians, but for *all*.

I want the Dancing Brothers to grow up in that future.

A tourist photographs "Spy Boy" Keith of the Wild Tchoupitoulas (2013).

Acknowledgments

This book is dedicated to Helen Hill, Dinerral Shavers, Wendy Byrne, and Magnolia Shorty, who all loved and embraced New Orleans to the fullest, but whose lives were cut short by violence. They are emblematic of all that is good and bad in this city.

First and foremost I would like to thank my husband Mark McGrain for his unwavering support and encouragement of my career. Besides sticking by me through thick and thin, his feedback on this book was invaluable.

I would never have been able to create so many images if it were not for the longtime working relationships with *Gambit* and Renaissance Publishing. I am very grateful to *Gambit* publishers Margo and Clancy DuBos for their outstanding dedication to providing our city with a fine weekly paper and a wonderful outlet for my work. Equally, Renaissance Publishing publishers Todd Matherne and Errol Laborde have been instrumental in supporting my career for a couple of decades by publishing my work in many of their beautiful magazines, such as *New Orleans Magazine* and *Louisiana Life*.

I will forever be grateful to my mentors, Michael P. Smith, David Richmond, Matt Anderson, and Bonnie Warren.

From the moment I first saw Michael P. Smith's photographs, I knew exactly what I wanted to do. After I called him a half dozen times, he finally said I could carry his equipment. He taught me how to develop film and print in the darkroom, how to file my negatives, how to show respect when photographing Mardi Gras Indians, and most importantly, how to hit the ground when shots were fired. I will never be able to thank him enough for introducing me to the side of New Orleans that I didn't know existed.

David Richmond will always have a special place in my heart for all of the long coffee and tea breaks where he shared his love and knowledge of New Orleans and photography. Whenever I was in over my head on an assignment, he would come to my rescue and help me.

I am especially grateful to photographer Matt Anderson for encouraging me to continue seeking a publisher after my first round of rejections and showing me the importance of being a fly on the wall.

For her collaboration on a variety of projects, I would like to thank writer and author Bonnie Warren, who was especially helpful in showing me how to get a book done. She has also been invaluable as a friend.

Heartfelt appreciation to Chris Rose and Lolis Eric Elie for writing such insightful contributions. Their writings never cease to amaze me.

Special thanks to Evelyn Rosenthal for her editing skills and kind words of encouragement.

Finally, I am grateful to work with UL Press's James Wilson, the designer who has given this book its special form.

NEW ORLEANS
LIFE AND DEATH IN THE BIG EASY

Southern Decadence Parade, French Quarter (2007).

Zulu parade, Tremé (2015).

Southern Decadence (2010).

Spyboy Alphonse Feliciana of the Golden Blades at the funeral for Wild Magnolias Big Chief Bo Dollis (2015).

Southern Decadence parade, French Quarter (2001).

Mother's Day in Tremé (2005).

5

National Guardsman during post-Katrina fires (2005).

Lady Buckjumpers Social Aid and Pleasure Club secondline (2006).

*Mardi Gras Indian on
Super Sunday (2004).*

*St. Patrick's Day,
Irish Channel (2004).*

*Mardi Gras Indian Spy Boy Michael Tenner Jr.
of the Comanche Hunters at Jazz Fest (2008).*

Divine Ladies Social Aid and Pleasure Club Secondline (2007).

Mystic Krewe of St. Anne parade (2003).

Thoth rider (2006).

Zulu rider (2003).

Southern Decadence parade (2002).

Mardi Gras day (2006).

13

Veterans Don Lassere and Stanley DiGiovanni at the
National WWII Museum, Veterans Day (2003).

Mardi Gras Indian Big Chief "Lil" Walter Cook of the Creole Wild West on the first anniversary of Hurricane Katrina (2006).

Red Dress Run (2013).

*Bernie Y. Miller and her daughter Juanita Miller lead the secondline as part of
Bethany United Methodist Church's Pentecost celebration (2002).*

16

Women parade in Krewe of Allah parade in Algiers (2008).

Women parade in secondline for HBO show Treme (2010).

Mardi Gras Indians in Lower 9th Ward (2006).

Saints fans (2004).

Arthur Jones and Wyatt Diaz graduate top of class at John McDonogh High School (2005).

Little Bo Peep, Southern Decadence, French Quarter (2002).

Archbishop Alfred Hughes, St. Joseph's Day at St. Louis Cathedral (2007).

Black Men of Labor Secondline (2010).

The Pussyfooters dance and march group (2013).

Calliope Highsteppers Social Aid and Pleasure Club Sunday secondline (2001).

Macedonia Baptist Church on the occasion of the church's 101st Anniversary (2002).

Downtown street party (2005).

Uptown garden party (2007).

Uptown Mardi Gras parade (2004).

Uptown garden party (2007).

Shamarr Allen (2012).

Father Pedro Nunez (2004).

Migrant workers seeking jobs during the rebuilding after Hurricane Katrina (2007).

Shipyard laborers (2004).

Cooks on a break in the French Quarter (2014).

Black Men of Labor's Social Aid and Pleasure Club (2006).

Roller Derby girl, Running of the Bulls (2013).

Wild Man of Fi Yi Yi, Super Sunday (2013).

7th Ward (2012).

FEMA trailer park (2006).

French Quarter (2014).

Central City (2014).

Dr. Ronald French reigns as Rex (2007).

Cedric Givens reigns as Zulu king (2013).

Tomato Fest queen gets crowned in Chalmette (2002).

Wild Tchoupitoulas Spy Girl Bryian Fluker gets crowned (2005).

Fancy hairdo in Tremé (2005).

*Drag Queen Bianca Del Rio
in French Quarter (2006).*

Mother's Day in Tremé (2005).

Ballet fundraiser (2009).

Saints fan's beard (2010).

Saints fan's hairdo (2010).

Delafose Brothers at Jazz Fest (2007).

Washboard hairdo in Tremé (2010).

Tuba in Central City secondline (2006).

Hairdo in Tremé (2002).

Troy "Trombone Shorty" Andrews (1993).

Troy "Trombone Shorty" Andrews (2013).

Kermit Ruffins (1995).

Kermit Ruffins (2005).

44

Kermit Ruffins at Sidney's Saloon in the 7th Ward (2010).

Holy Cross Marching Band in Uptown parade (2004).

Jazz Funeral in Central City (2007).

Preservation Hall Band (2004).

Rebirth Brass Band at Maple Leaf Bar (2005).

Secondline in jazz funeral for photographer Herman Leonard (2010).

Secondline in jazz funeral for photographer Herman Leonard (2010).

Secondline dancer, 7th Ward (2006).

Secondline in French Quarter, featuring Darryl "Dancing Man 504" Young (2011).

Secondline dancer at "Silence is Violence" celebration (2010).

Andrew Gerber and Savion Riggs dancing in Marigny (2009).

"Save Charity" hospital secondline (2009).

Woman in hair rollers, Central City (2011).

Woman in hair rollers in Krewe Delusion parade, Marigny (2012).

Estabon Eugene (center), known as Chief Peppy of the Golden Eagles Uptown tribe (2005).

Secondline in Central City (2003).

Men play tambourines in French Quarter for Mardi Gras (2004).

Secondline in Marigny Triangle (2011).

Oz dance club on Bourbon Street (2003).

Bounce party with Big Freedia at the Republic (2013).

Bustout Burlesque at House of Blues (2008).

Bounce party at the Republic (2013).

Flag girl performs during Zulu parade (2009).

Amanda Shaw performs at Mid-city Rock 'n Bowl (2003).

A woman flashes her breasts on Bourbon Street during Mardi Gras (2006).

A man flashes his chest under the Claiborne overpass on Mardi Gras day (2009).

Zulu parade participant (2007).   *French Quarter mime (2000).*

Krewe du Vieux parade reveler costumed as fictional character Ignatius Reilly from John Kennedy Toole's A Confederacy of Dunces (2004).

Lucky Dog man reminiscent of fictional character Ignatius Reilly (2000).

Sudan Social Aid and Pleasure Club secondliner (2006).

Mystic Krewe of Barkus parade participant (2008).

A dog costumed as Mr. Okra in the Mystic Krewe of Barkus parade (2015).

Arthur "Mr. Okra" Robinson, the roving produce vendor (2009).

Two men with their dogs after a secondline in Tremé (2010).

A couple with their dogs during the Barkus parade in the French Quarter (2012).

Mardi Gras horseman in Garden District (2013).

Horseman in funeral for Darnell Mitchell "Homeboy" Stewart in Tremé (2009).

Nutria bounty hunter (2009).

Becky Verret plays with her three-week-old nutria "Shaggy" (2002).

Alligator farmer Harvey Kleibert (2001).

Chef John Besh during a frogging trip (2005).

Man with a snake on Frenchmen Street (2010).

Woman with snake in Tremé (2009).

Sleeping at Zulu parade (2009).

Sleeping at Iris parade (2009).

Bounty hunter Chris Meyers and wife Trisha Meyers kiss (2007).

St. Patrick's Day paradegoer receives a kiss (2012).

Mardi Gras revelers kiss (2014).

Jazz Fest attendees kiss (2010).

Marie and Caryl Fagot prepare their annual St. Joseph's Day Altar (2005).

*Willie Mae Seaton and granddaughter Kerry Seaton-Blackman
at Willie Mae's Scotch House in Tremé (2005).*

Galatoire's, Downtown (2008).

Camellia Grill, Uptown (2009).

Crawfish Boil (2003).

Crawfish Boil (2008).

Mimi's in the Marigny bar (2005).

Gumbo party in the French Quarter (2006).

Patron party for the Ogden Museum of Southern Art (2013).

Art gallery opening in Bywater (2014).

Street flooding in Lower Garden District (2003).

Jazz Fest (2013).

A member of the Sudan Social Aid and Pleasure Club leads the Rebirth Brass Band (2007).

Rockers Sean Yseult and Chris Lee secondline through the French Quarter after their wedding (2008).

Jack Radosta protesting as George W. Bush's presidential motorcade passes
on the second anniversary of Hurricane Katrina (2007).

New Orleans Saints fans celebrate the team's Super Bowl victory in the French Quarter (2010).

Maverick Ancar, a football player for Port Sulfur High School, looks at his home floating in a canal (2006).

Drew Brees poses for photos after a playoff win in route to the Super Bowl (2010).

Roselle and Tavish McGrain after heavy rain caused street flooding in the Lower Garden District (2002).

Man paddles with dogs in Bayou St. John (2009).

Boy running through water at rainy Jazz Fest (2008).

Man running on Canal Street during the height of Hurricane Katrina (2005).

Children at the Uptown Jewish Community Center (2003).

Children in the 7th Ward (2007).

Students at John McDonogh High School (2013).

Students at Lusher Charter School (2014).

New Orleans police officers search a teen (2004).

Police officers prepare to search a student at John McDonogh High School (2006).

Protesters and educators clash at school board meeting (2004).

Protester and gay man clash on Bourbon Street (2005).

Congresswoman Lindy Boggs shares a laugh with a veteran at the National WWII Museum (2003).

"Papa" Joe Glasper shares a laugh with a patron at his bar Joe's Cozy Corner (2004).

Lines of evacuees crowd the interstate one day before Hurricane Katrina (2005).

Lines of stranded people at the Louisiana Superdome one day before Hurricane Katrina (2005).

Residents seeking shelter at the Louisiana Superdome one day before Hurricane Katrrina (2005).

Residents seeking shelter at the Louisiana Superdome one day before Hurricane Katrrina (2005).

Hardin Tutt, homeless after Katrina, camps in front of City Hall (2007).

Randy Padick from Illinois camps in City Park as he waits for Katrina clean-up work (2005).

Homeless (2011).

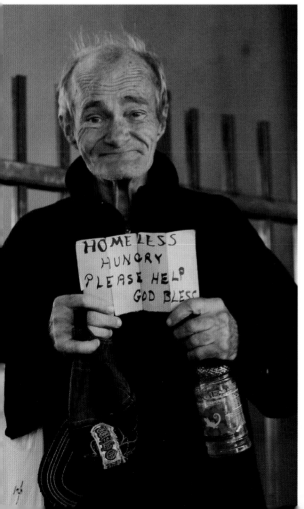

Bourbon Street after Saints win Super Bowl (2010).

A young man during "Hands Up, Don't Shoot" protest (2014).

Supporters of the Danziger Seven chant as charged officers turn themselves in at the city jail (2007).

Music fans at Voodoo Music Experience (2003).

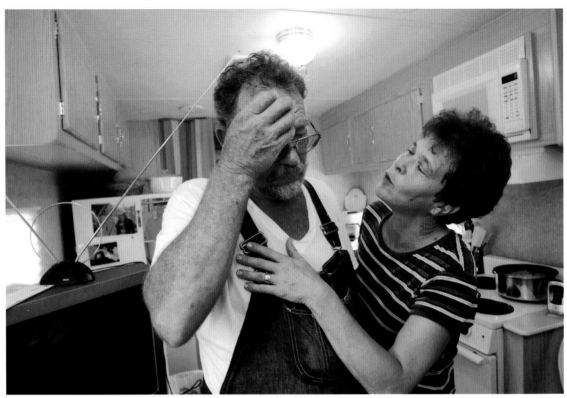

Donald and Colleen Bordelon in FEMA trailer outside of their Arabi home (2006).

Smith family lives in a FEMA trailer, Belle Chasse (2006).

Mary Burns protests the Army Corps of Engineers at a memorial on the first anniversary of Hurricane Katrina (2006).

Revelers mock the Army Corps of Engineers (2006).

President Barack Obama listens to nine-year-old Tyren Scott's question at UNO (2009).

President George W. Bush at the National D-Day Museum (2004).

Delegates applaud Sarah Palin at the Southern Republican Leadership Conference (2010).

Audience cheers during introduction of Hillary Clinton at Sen. Mary Landrieu rally (2014).

Richard Lindsey waits at the Common Ground Health Clinic,
which provided free health care to patients (2007).

Cindy West yells her protests to the Affordable Care Act during a health care town hall meeting hosted by Louisiana Sen. David Vitter (2009).

NOPD officer Michael Hunter, one of the Danziger Seven, gets a hug after turning himself in after state indictments for attempted murder for the shooting of civilians during the aftermath of Katrina (2007).

Outgoing Mayor Ray Nagin hugs incoming Mayor Mitch Landrieu at inauguration (2010).

Mayor Ray Nagin greets supporter in the Lower 9th Ward neighborhood (2003).

Former Mayor Ray Nagin after a jury delivered a guilty verdict for corruption charges (2014).

Canal Street madam Jeanette Maier (2002).

David Vitter talks about family values (2004).

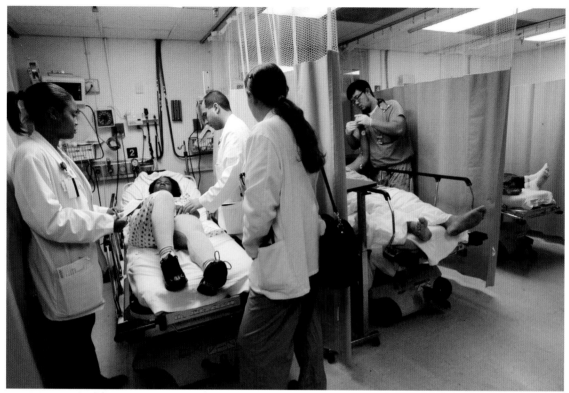

Charity Hospital (2004).

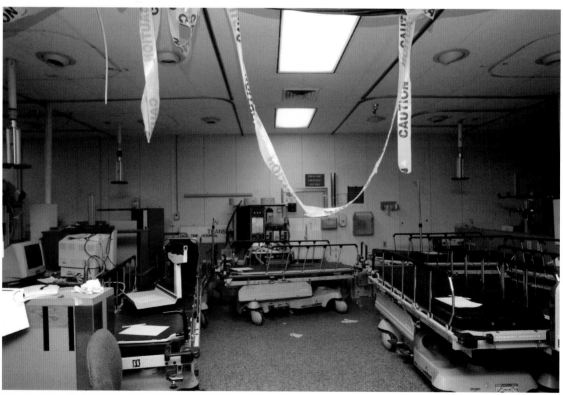

Charity Hospital (2007).

Two men in front of closed Charity Hospital (2009).

White house, Uptown (2009).

White house, Lower 9th Ward (2007).

"Little Pink House" during Hurricane Katrina (2005).

Brad Pitt's Make It Right Foundation's art installation "Pink Houses" (2007).

Lower 9th Ward (2007).

Make It Right Houses in the Lower 9th Ward (2009).

NEXT PAGE: *St. Roch neighborhood (2007).*   119

St. Thomas Housing Projects (1996).

River Gardens where St. Thomas Housing Projects once stood (2009).

Lafitte Housing Projects on Orleans Avenue (2002).

Lafitte Housing Projects on Orleans Avenue after demolition (2009).

St. Roch Market (2002).

St. Roch Market (2015).

Habitat for Humanity volunteers raise roof in the Musicians Village in Upper 9th Ward (2007).

Tremé Sidewalk Steppers dance on rooftop (2012).

Hearse on neutral ground right after Katrina, rusted Superdome in background (2005).

"Thou Shalt Not Kill" sign right after Katrina, rusted Superdome in background (2005).

Blighted Joy Theater (2008).

Restored Joy Theater (2012).

NEXT PAGE: *Restored Saenger Theater (2014).*   131

Christmas, Lower 9th Ward (2005).

Christmas, Lakeview (2005).

FEMA trailer, Christmas (2005).

Chris Williams and Danielle Miles light candles at a vigil in Jackson Square marking the second anniversary of Hurricane Katrina (2007).

AT LEFT: *Voodoo ceremony to ward off hurricanes just weeks prior to Hurricane Katrina (2005).*

Ashaun Cotton, Debera Jefferson, and her grandchildren listen to Rev. Aldon Cotton preach to his congregation about surviving day to day after Hurricane Katrina (2006).

Mourners grieve the loss of Dinerral Shavers, snare drummer for the Hot 8 Brass Band and music teacher at L.E. Rabouin High School (2007).

Mount Carmel student Crisina Hnatyshyn gets a welcome hug from Sister Camille Campbell on the first day back to school after Katrina (2006).

Patrina Peters hugs Geneva Seals during a memorial ceremony on the third anniversary of Hurricane Katrina in the Lower 9th Ward of New Orleans (2008).

New Orleans police officers pepper spray and taser protesters demonstrating against the demolition of housing projects in the city (2007).

Dancing at the Maple Leaf Bar (2008).

Young women in Tremé watch the police go by (2005).

Transgender woman talks to police at Gay Easter Parade (2013).

A man goes to Central Lockup (2004).

A tourist parties on Bourbon Street (2006).

Man is arrested at a parade Uptown (2004).

Man is arrested at a parade Downtown (2011).

A woman looks through window as police make an arrest in Central City (2004).

A woman dancing in window on Bourbon Street (2002).

A murder victim lies on the ground in the Lower Garden District (2007).

A man is arrested in the French Quarter (2007).

A drunk man lies on the ground in the French Quarter (2009).

Bystanders tend to a female protester after she was tased and pepper-sprayed by New Orleans police officers (2007).

Paradegoers tend to two women shot during the Muses parade on St. Charles Avenue (2004).

St. Louis Cathedral (2011).

Greater Full Gospel Church in Central City (2014).

153

Voodoo on the Bayou Ceremony by Voodoo Priestess Sallie Glassman (2011).

Jazz funeral secondline for Joe Finch, Faubourg Marigny (2015).

Buffalo Soldiers and friends ride horses at funeral for Darnell "Homeboy" Mitchell Stewart (2014).

NOPD mounted police at funeral for Archbishop Philip Hannan (2011).

A grave digger at Holt Cemetery (2003).

Artists Jeffrey Holmes and Andrea Garland create memorial in Bywater after Katrina (2005).

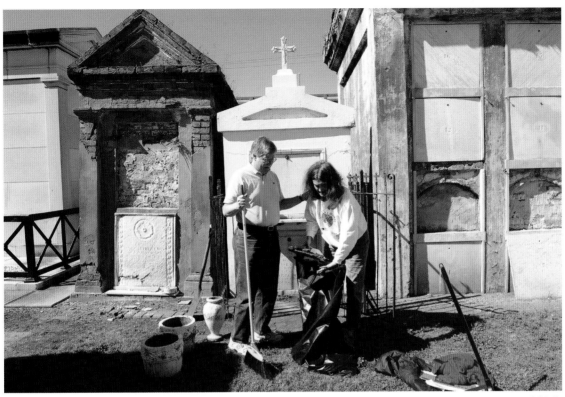

Tending the family tomb at St. Louis No. 2 Cemetery (2014).

Tending the family grave in Holt Cemetery (2014).

Metairie Cemetery (2004).

NEXT PAGE: *Holt Cemetery (2008).* 161

Funeral for famed jazz musician Harold Dejan, St. Louis No. 3 Cemetery (2002).

Funeral for oil tycoon Patrick Taylor, French Quarter (2004).

Funeral for slain rapper Magnolia Shorty, Central City (2010).

Funeral for Archbishop Philip Hannan, French Quarter (2011).

Mourners carry the casket of Hot 8 Brass Band drummer Dinerral Shavers (2007).

Musicians follow hearse for slain filmmaker Helen Hill (2007).

"Big Chief" Monk Boudreaux and other Mardi Gras Indians follow the hearse of "Big Chief" Bo Dollis (2015).

Krewe of Barkus parade, French Quarter (2013).

Funeral in Tremé (2014).

171

Mourners follow hearse in funeral for Congresswoman Lindy Boggs (2013).

Mourners follow hearse in funeral for Darnell Mitchell "Homeboy" Stewart (2004).

"Kill Cops" graffiti on stop sign at murder scene in the 7th Ward (2014).

"You Will Die" graffiti at murder scene in Central City (2004).

A woman collapses at murder scene in the 7th Ward (2014).

A young woman weeps at a murder scene in Gentilly (2009).

Lead prosecutor Bobbi Bernstein hugs Lance Madison, brother of victim Ronald Madison, after the jury delivered guilty verdicts for five of the "Danziger Seven" police officers (2011).

Mourners hug at funeral (2007).

Two women embrace near a murder scene in Gentilly (2009).

Two men embrace at the murder scene of victim Helen Hill (2006).

179

*Vigil for three employees killed at the Louisiana Pizza Kitchen
in the French Quarter (1996).*

A woman sings at a vigil for murder victim Wendy Byrne, a popular French Quarter bartender (2009).

Jazz funeral for "Big Chief" Allison "Tootie" Montana (2005).

Jazz funeral for Helen Hill (2007).

Dinerral Shavers (56 on jersey) in secondline, one year before being shot to death, Uptown (2005).

NEXT PAGE: *Jazz funeral for Dinerral Shavers, Central City,
amid Hurricane Katrina rebuilding (2007).*

Funeral for Congresswoman Lindy Boggs at St. Louis Cathedral (2013).

Funeral in Holt Cemetery (2014).

Jazz funeral for Helen Hill (2007).

Spyboy Ricky Gettridge escorts Resa Bazile, aka Baby Doll Cinnamon Black, at Jazz funeral for Treme Brass Band bass drummer "Uncle" Lionel Batiste (2012).

Jazz funeral for "Uncle" Lionel Batiste (2012).

Travis "Trumpet Black" Hill performs at Jazz Fest (2013).

Funeral for Travis "Trumpet Black" Hill (2015).

Travis "Trumpet Black" Hill performs at Jackson Square (1996).

Travis "Trumpet Black" Hill funeral (2015).

Socialite Mickey Easterling sitting up at her funeral at the Saenger Theater (2014).

A mannequin of late R&B singer Ernie K-Doe at the Mother-in-Law Lounge in the 7th Ward (2009).

Wild Man Mardi Gras Indian suit left in the 7th Ward after Katrina (2005).

Zulu member on Jackson Avenue on Mardi Gras (2013).

Jesus statue with oil line after Hurricane Katrina, Chalmette (2005).

Reflection of Jesus statute on rear of St. Louis Cathedral (2015).

A memorial funeral procession for the Lower 9th Ward on third anniversary of Hurricane Katrina (2008).

A memorial jazz funeral in the French Quarter (2014).

Enough! sign at murder site in Marigny (2007).

Love sign near St. Louis Cemetery No. 2 (2014).

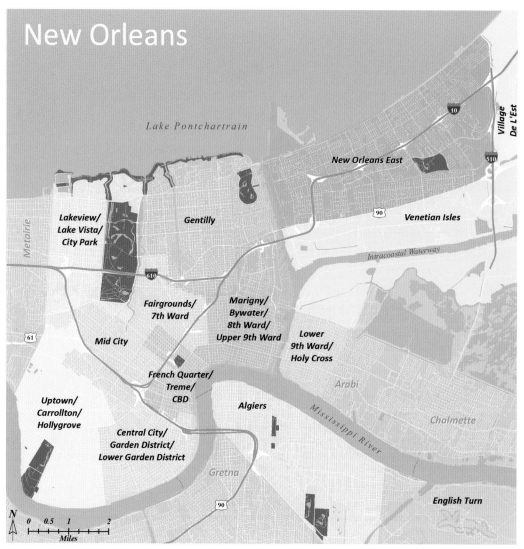

New Orleans

Lake Pontchartrain

Metairie

Lakeview/
Lake Vista/
City Park

Gentilly

New Orleans East

Village
De L'Est

Venetian Isles

Intracoastal Waterway

Fairgrounds/
7th Ward

Marigny/
Bywater/
8th Ward/
Upper 9th Ward

Lower
9th Ward/
Holy Cross

Mid City

French Quarter/
Treme/
CBD

Arabi

Mississippi River

Chalmette

Uptown/
Carrollton/
Hollygrove

Algiers

Central City/
Garden District/
Lower Garden District

Gretna

English Turn

N

0   0.5   1   2
Miles

"City of New Orleans, US Census" by Aimee Preau.

GLOSSARY

7th Ward, 8th Ward, and 9th Ward are neighborhoods sometimes called "the back of town," and are generally poor or working class sections that were hit very hard during Katrina. While there has been some gentrification since the storm, overall recovery has been slow.

Army Corps of Engineers is the federal agency responsible for such public works as levees, dams, canals, and flood protection. The agency was largely blamed for the devastation caused when the levees broke during Hurricane Katrina.

Baby Dolls is one of the first women's organizations to mask and perform during Mardi Gras, tracing their origins from Storyville-era brothels and dance halls to their re-emergence in post-Katrina New Orleans.

Barkus, aka The Mystic Krewe of Barkus, first paraded in 1994. It is an annual Mardi Gras event that promotes animal adoption and rescue of homeless animals. Barkus is the only Mardi Gras "krewe" in New Orleans created for dogs.

Black Men of Labor Social Aid and Pleasure Club was formed in 1993 after the death of traditional jazz musician and mentor Danny Barker, who introduced many young African American musicians to brass band music and the practice of playing a jazz funeral through the Fairview Baptist Church. The members of BMOL pay homage to men who work and include musicians, community activists, and many other working men.

Lindy Boggs (Marie Corinne Morrison Claiborne Boggs) represented New Orleans in Congress from the time of her husband Hale Boggs's disappearance and presumed death in 1973 until 1991.

Bounce music is an energetic style of New Orleans hip hop music which is said to have originated as early as the late 1980s. Bounce is characterized by call and response style party and Mardi Gras Indian chants and dance call-outs that are frequently hypersexual.

Central City is the predominantly African American neighborhood located at the lower end of Uptown, just above the Central Business District, important in the city's brass band and Mardi Gras Indian traditions.

Chalmette is a predominately white suburb in St. Bernard Parish located east of New Orleans on the Mississippi River where the Battle of New Orleans was fought in 1815.

Charity Hospital, founded in 1736 as a hospital for the poor, was closed after Katrina despite much protest and controversy, leaving many New Orleanians without healthcare.

Glossary

Danziger 7 refers to seven police officers indicted for shootings that took place on September 4, 2005, at the Danziger Bridge six days after Katrina, killing two citizens and severely wounding four others. On August 5, 2011, a federal jury in New Orleans convicted five police officers of multiple charges related to the cover-up and deprivation of civil rights. However, the convictions were vacated on September 17, 2013, due to prosecutorial misconduct and a new trial was ordered.

FEMA trailers are the manufactured trailers that the federal government supplied to Katrina victims after the historic storm. They were intended to serve as intermediate term shelter after a disaster.

Flambeaux carriers served as beacons for paradegoers to better enjoy the spectacle of night festivities. The first flambeaux carriers were slaves. Many view the flambeaux as a kind of performance art and viewers often throw money their way.

Frenchmen Street is most famous for the three-block section in the Faubourg Marigny that is home to some of the city's most popular live music venues, including Snug Harbor, The Spotted Cat, and The Maison in addition to restaurants, bars, bookstores, coffee shops, and other businesses.

Joe "Papa Joe" Glasper, owner/proprietor of the famous Tremé club "Joe's Cozy Corner," died in April, 2005, in the Orleans Parish Jail shortly after being convicted of manslaughter for shooting a patron in his bar.

Helen Hill was a thirty-six-year-old filmmaker killed by an unidentified intruder she encountered in the early morning on January 4, 2007. Her husband, who was holding their baby, was also shot three times. Her death (one of six murders in the city that day), coupled with the murder a week before of beloved musician Dinerral Shavers, sparked civic outrage. Thousands marched against the rampant violence in post-Katrina New Orleans. This "March Against Violence on City Hall" drew significant press coverage throughout the United States and beyond.

Holt Cemetery is a potters field cemetery located next to Delgado Community College in Mid-City that was established in 1879 to inter the city's poorest residents, as it continues to do today. Legendary trumpeter Charles "Buddy" Bolden is said to be buried there.

Ignatius Reilly, the main character in the Pulitzer-prize winning novel *A Confederacy of Dunces* by John Kennedy Toole, is described as a modern Don Quixote, eccentric, idealistic, sometimes to the point of delusion. A statue of the famous New Orleans fictional character who sold Lucky Dogs in the French Quarter sits in the 800 block of Canal Street.

Jazz funeral begins with a march by the family, friends, and a brass band from the home, funeral home, or church to the cemetery. Throughout the march, the band plays somber dirges and hymns until a change in the tenor of the ceremony takes place after either the deceased is en-

Glossary

tombed, or the hearse leaves the procession and members of the procession say their final goodbye and "cut the body loose."

Krewe is an organization that puts on a parade or ball for the Carnival season.

Krewe Delusion, founded in 2010, is a satirical parade that follows Krewe du Vieux.

Krewe du Vieux, established in 1987, is a Carnival krewe that parades through the Faubourg Marigny neighborhood and meanders through the French Quarter. One of the earliest parades of the Carnival calendar, the parade is noted for wild satirical and adult themes.

Lower 9th Ward is one of the neighborhoods hardest hit by Hurricane Katrina when the federal levee wall, built by the Army Corps of Engineers, next to the Industrial Canal broke causing total flooding and devastation. Recovery of the neighborhood ten years after Katrina remains slow, though the new Make It Right homes built by Brad Pitt's foundation have made the neighborhood a tourist destination.

Magnolia Shorty, the stage name for Renetta Yemika Lowe-Bridgewater, was a rapper in the New Orleans-based bounce music scene. One of the first women signed to Cash Money Records, she was considered a legend of bounce music at the time of her death. On December 20, 2010, she was shot twenty-six times in a drive-by shooting while sitting in her car in the apartment complex where she lived. Her funeral was attended by many notable rappers including Lil Wayne and Juvenile.

Make It Right Foundation was founded by Brad Pitt in 2007 to aid in the environmentally friendly rebuilding of the Lower 9th Ward after Hurricane Katrina, vowing to build 150 sustainable homes for former residents.

Mardi Gras Indians, originating in the early to mid-nineteenth century, are African American revelers who dress up for Mardi Gras in hand-sewn suits that pay homage to Native Americans who helped slaves. Many different tribes also parade on St. Joseph's Day (March 19th) and the nearest Sunday, better known as Super Sunday. Spy Boy, Flag Boy, and Big Chiefs are different ranks within a tribe.

Marigny, also called Faubourg Marigny, just east and adjacent to the French Quarter, was laid out during the early part of the nineteenth century by eccentric Creole millionaire developer Bernard Xavier Phillipe de Marigny de Mandeville, and is known for its Spanish and French colonial architecture and its artists community. The Marigny is also where world-famous Frenchmen Street is located.

Ray Nagin, mayor of New Orleans when Katrina struck in 2005, and later reelected in 2006 despite his unpopularity due to his infamous "Chocolate City" speech which created a racial firestorm. In 2014, Nagin was convicted on twenty of twenty-one charges of wire fraud, bribery and money laundering related to bribes from city contractors before and after Hurricane Katrina and was sentenced to ten years in federal prison.

Mr. Okra, whose real name is Arthur Robinson, is known as the roving produce vendor who has become a local celebrity in recent years for his deep bellowing voice amplified through a megaphone which can be heard throughout neighborhoods, calling out "I've got strawberries and bananas, sweeeet peaches and broccoli."

Nutria, also known as a river rat, is a large, semi-aquatic rodent with orange teeth, whose feeding and burrowing behaviors destroy protective levees, making this invasive species a pest throughout most of south Louisiana. Bounties were paid for tails of nutria to try to eradicate them.

Phunny Phorty Phellows, who first took to the streets in 1878 (with a long break that lasted from 1898 until 1981), is known for its satirical parades and marks the beginning of Carnival season. Krewe members, often dressed in costumes that reflect topical issues, ride a streetcar from Uptown to Downtown, drinking champagne, eating king cake, and throwing the first beads of the Carnival season

Red Dress Run, sponsored by the Hash House Harriers, a self-proclaimed "drinking club with a running problem," the Annual Red Dress Run winds through the French Quarter and Downtown in August, raising funds for local charities.

Rex, founded in 1872, is a Carnival krewe that stages one of the city's most celebrated parades on Mardi Gras day. Rex is Latin for "king" and Rex reigns as "The King of Carnival."

Running of the Bulls coincides with the world-famous San Fermin Festival in Pamplona, Spain. The annual summer event has mushroomed to include thousands of participants since it was first staged in 2007. Instead of being chased by bulls, runners are chased by roller derby girls wielding wiffle bats to whack the rear ends of runners.

St. Joseph's Day is a city-wide event featuring public and private altars of food and drink commemorating the relief St. Joseph provided during the famine in Sicily. Not just for Italian-Americans anymore, the food is shared with visitors and generally distributed to charity after the altar is dismantled.

St. Patrick's Day is celebrated throughout the city with major parades in Irish Channel, Bywater, and French Quarter neighborhoods, including a combined Irish-Italian Parade celebrating both St. Patrick's Day and St. Joseph's Day. In the spirit of Mardi Gras, the Irish Channel parade is famous for throwing onions, carrots, cabbages, potatoes, and other ingredients for making an Irish strew.

St. Roch is a neighborhood in the 8th Ward centered along St. Roch Avenue, known for its St. Roch Cemeteries and the St. Roch Market.

Glossary

Secondline is a tradition in a brass band parade that occurs on most Sundays between October and March. The "first line" is the main section of the parade, or the members of the actual club with the parading permit as well as the brass band, followed by revelers who enjoy the music, called the "second line."

Dinerral Shavers, an educator and best known as the drummer for the Hot 8 Brass Band, died from a gunshot to the back of his head while driving his family. He was not the intended target and his murder, along with a spate of other similar crimes that week, sparked a massive protest at City Hall in 2007.

Silence is Violence is a campaign for peace through community outreach and education, founded in 2007 following the murders of musician Dinerral Shavers and filmmaker Helen Hill.

Social Aid and Pleasure Clubs can be traced back to nineteenth-century benevolent societies that provided health care and burial services for their members. Besides these benefits, the clubs also encouraged leadership skills and provided a space for discussing social issues, as well as entertainment in the form of picnics, annual Sunday parades, dinners, and balls.

Southern Decadence is an annual six-day event held by the gay and lesbian community during Labor Day Weekend, climaxing with a parade through the French Quarter on the Sunday before Labor Day.

Super Sunday is the most significant day for the Mardi Gras Indians, besides Mardi Gras Day. The New Orleans Mardi Gras Indian Council usually holds its Indian Sunday on the third Sunday of March, around St. Joseph's Day, when the Mardi Gras Indians once again dress in their feathers and suits and take to the streets to meet other "gangs."

Tremé, pronounced trə-MAY, one of the oldest neighborhoods in New Orleans, directly north, and adjacent to the French Quarter, was the main neighborhood of free people of color. Despite recent gentrification, Tremé continues to be a racially mixed neighborhood, an important center of the city's African American and Creole culture, especially the modern brass band tradition. HBO created a four-season television series called *Treme* by David Simon that highlighted the events after Katrina.

Uptown affluent section of New Orleans that runs along St. Charles Avenue and contains a wealth of nineteenth-century architecture. Tulane and Loyola Universities, as well as Audubon Park, are located here.

Zulu Social Aid & Pleasure Club, founded in 1916, is a Carnival krewe most famous for its Zulu parade on Mardi Gras morning. Zulu is New Orleans's largest predominantly African American Carnival organization, and is known for its blackfaced krewe members wearing grass skirts and its extremely coveted hand-painted coconuts.

ABOUT THE PHOTOGRAPHER

Cheryl Gerber is a freelance journalist and documentary photographer working in New Orleans, where she was born. She began her journalism career as a reporter but switched to photography after spending a year working in Honduras. In 1992, she began working for Michael P. Smith, who nurtured her desire to document daily life in New Orleans. Today, she is a regular contributor to *The New York Times*, the Associated Press, and *New Orleans Magazine*, and has been a staff photographer for *Gambit Weekly* since 1994. During the past two decades, Cheryl has won several awards from the New Orleans Press Club for her work on social issues and news photography.

To view more of Cheryl's work, visit: www.cherylgerberphotography.com

Photo by Andrew Gerber.